Dear Parents:

These books are written for ages 3–8 with a primary goal of welcoming children to the wonderful world of literature. Younger age groups enjoy these stories by listening to the readings while kindergarteners often attempt these books on their own.

For early readers the first steps into that world can be very frightening. It is new, and scary and challenges their confidence. "The Adventures of Prank" were created to help. Each story is very short, as short as the attention span of this age group.

Each story has a defined ending, giving the reader a sense of a task accomplished. The structure of the text uses tools that are easily accessible to children at this age: pattern recognition, grouping and rhythm

visit www.kcdeli

D1198618

Adventure of Prank the cat

Meet Prank

By K.C. Light   Pictures by Elena Mogi

Prank is an adorable, lovable cat. Rescued from a shelter at an early age, he now spends his days eating, sleeping and getting up to mischief.

He thinks he is Siamese, because it sounds cool and boosts his confidence. He is still a bit shy, but is very kind and sweet. Usually he is well behaved but sometimes he gets up to no good.

His antics are documented here in a series of anecdotes.

K.C. Light

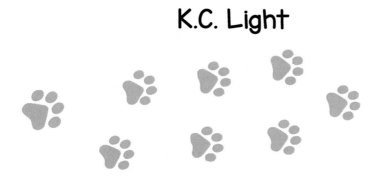

Hi! My name is Prank
(not Frank)
and I'm a cat
Please take note of that

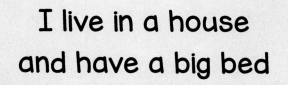

I live in a house
and have a big bed

My home is warm
and very bright
I play a lot
- mostly at night

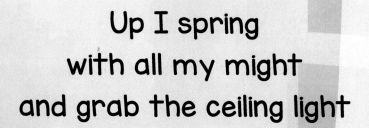

Up I spring
with all my might
and grab the ceiling light

I make as much noise
as I possibly can
and then…
I do it over again

"It is midnight Prank,
you crazy cat" - my owner
often says

I am not crazy - I object
I am NOCTURNAL

Now to the sock drawer
All socks to the floor!

Then to the drapes I fly !

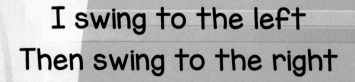

I swing to the left
Then swing to the right

Oh...what a delight !
At the highest of heights

It is so much fun
to play at night !

Beep ! Beep ! Beep !
The alarm goes off
and off I go... in fright !

I land on the floor
On all fours
and hide well out of sight

- Prank, what's going on ?
- Nothing, absolutely nothing

THE END

OUTTAKES